Garbage Trucks

Julie Murray

Abdo
Kids

MY COMMUNITY: VEHICLES

abdopublishing.com

Published by Abdo Kids, a division of ABDO, PO Box 398166, Minneapolis, Minnesota 55439.
Copyright © 2016 by Abdo Consulting Group, Inc. International copyrights reserved in all countries.
No part of this book may be reproduced in any form without written permission from the publisher.

Printed in the United States of America, North Mankato, Minnesota.

102015

012016

 THIS BOOK CONTAINS
RECYCLED MATERIALS

Photo Credits: iStock, Shutterstock

Production Contributors: Teddy Borth, Jennie Forsberg, Grace Hansen

Design Contributors: Candice Keimig, Dorothy Toth

Library of Congress Control Number: 2015941778

Cataloging-in-Publication Data

Murray, Julie.
 Garbage trucks / Julie Murray.
   p. cm. -- (My community: vehicles)
ISBN 978-1-68080-130-9
Includes index.
1. Refuse collection vehicles--Juvenile literature. I. Title.
628.4/42--dc23
                          2015941778

Table of Contents

Garbage Truck

Abby puts out the trash.

Here comes the truck!

The truck is big.

It has big wheels.

The driver sits in the **cab**.

She drives the truck.

103132

SAFETY NOTICE
AVISO DE SEGURIDAD

WM
WASTE MANAGEMENT

Think Green.

USDOT 1967746

XPEDITOR

The truck stops.

It picks up the trash.

A lift **loads** the trash.

It goes into the bin.

13

Some trucks **load** in the back.

Others load in the front.

Some load from the side.

The trash gets **crushed**.

Now more can fit!

The truck goes to the dump.

It unloads the trash.

Have you seen a garbage truck?

Parts of a Garbage Truck

bin

lift

cab

wheels

Glossary

cab
where the driver sits in a truck.

crush
to press with a force that destroys.

load
to bring in.

Index

abdokids.com

Use this code to log on to abdokids.com and access crafts, games, videos, and more!

Abdo Kids Code:
MGK1309